Wid

Clicquot

The Historical Truth Behind the Movie

ELLA SNOW PUBLISHING

Copyright

Disclaimer

This book, "Widow Clicquot: The Historical Truth Behind the Movie," seeks to provide a thorough investigation of the historical events and individuals featured in the film "Widow Clicquot." While every effort has been made to verify the accuracy of the historical facts presented, readers should be aware that some interpretations and analyses are dependent on the author's perspective and the sources accessible at the time of writing.

The book covers both verifiable historical facts and the dramatic components depicted in the film. The film itself may take artistic liberties for narrative and entertainment purposes, therefore certain events, dialogues, and characterizations may not accurately mirror historical occurrences. This book aims to highlight these disparities and provide context where needed.

Readers should also be aware that historical study is a constantly growing field. New discoveries or interpretations may emerge, altering our understanding of the events portrayed in this book. As a result, this book represents the author's best attempt to offer accurate information using the knowledge and sources accessible at the time of writing.

Table Of Contents

Contents

Contents

Introduction

"The only thing that should ever come between a woman and her goals is a corkscrew." This funny yet powerful phrase perfectly depicts the attitude of Barbe-Nicole Ponsardin Clicquot, the protagonist of the captivating film "Widow Clicquot." Based on Tilar J. Mazzeo's book, the film brings audiences to the early nineteenth century, where a young widow defies traditional expectations to establish one of the world's most prominent champagne houses.

Barbe-Nicole Ponsardin, born in 1777, married François Clicquot, the heir to a small winery business. Their original relationship was one of convenience, but it quickly developed into a partnership based on mutual respect and common goals. François recognized Barbe-Nicole's great commercial knowledge, which was uncommon and underrated in women of that age. They hoped to grow their small business into a well-known champagne establishment.

Tragedy came early in their marriage when François died unexpectedly, leaving Barbe-Nicole widowed at 27 years old. In an era when widows were expected to settle into calm domesticity, Barbe-Nicole's decision to take over her late husband's business was nothing short of revolutionary. Women faced a harsh commercial climate in the early 1800s, with legislative and societal barriers aimed at keeping them out of the market. Despite these hurdles, Barbe-Nicole went on a mission to realize the vision she and François had shared.

Barbe-Nicole's journey was riddled with challenges. The political situation in post-revolutionary France was volatile, and the economic landscape was similarly uncertain. The Napoleonic Wars disrupted commercial networks and caused financial turmoil. However, Barbe-Nicole's resolve grew stronger. She recognized that in order to flourish, her champagne needed to stand out not only in quality, but also in branding and originality.

Barbe-Nicole perfected the méthode champenoise, the traditional way of manufacturing sparkling wine, which was one of her most significant contributions to the champagne business. This intricate and labor-intensive procedure needed precision and patience. Barbe-Nicole's painstaking attention to detail guaranteed that every bottle of Veuve Clicquot champagne was of the finest quality. She created techniques that increased purity and taste, including as the riddling process, in which bottles were progressively turned and tilted to gather sediment in the neck for removal. This invention significantly increased the popularity and renown of her champagne.

Barbe-Nicole's economic plans were as audacious as her production methods. Recognizing the significance of branding, she insisted on the unique yellow label that became associated with Veuve Clicquot. This was a masterstroke at a time when visual identity was still a new notion in marketing. The yellow label distinguished her bottles from competitors, becoming a mark of excellence and elegance.

Her marketing expertise went beyond labels. Barbe-Nicole recognized the value of word-of-mouth and elite endorsements and developed contacts with significant persons around Europe. Her champagne was served at royal palaces and magnificent gatherings, generating international demand. The Widow Clicquot brand evolved from a product to a status symbol, representing luxury and revelry.

Barbe-Nicole's leadership extended to her employees. Unlike many business owners at the time, she instilled a sense of loyalty and dedication among her staff. She was noted for her fair treatment and the familial atmosphere she fostered in her workplace. This method not only increased production, but also assured that her employees were dedicated to upholding the high standards she established.

The Widow Clicquot's accomplishment was more than just a personal victory; it was a watershed event for women in business. Her accomplishments challenged the widespread belief that women were incapable of operating successful businesses. Her narrative inspired a generation of women to follow their dreams despite cultural restraints. Barbe-Nicole Ponsardin Clicquot became a symbol of possibility, demonstrating that with determination and vision, barriers might be overcome.

The film "Widow Clicquot" perfectly depicts the essence of Barbe-Nicole's journey. It's a narrative about love, loss, and unwavering determination. Barbe-Nicole is portrayed with depth and nuance by Haley Bennett, who highlights both her sensitivity and strength. The film's historical accuracy, paired with its captivating narrative, make it an effective tribute to a lady who altered the path of an industry.

Set against the magnificent background of the Champagne region, the film's cinematography is a visual feast. The beautiful vineyards and old cellars create a stunning visual backdrop for Barbe-Nicole's story. The vintage costumes and intricate settings transport spectators to a world on the verge of modernization, reflecting the excitement and uncertainty of the time.

The supporting cast, which includes Tom Sturridge as François Clicquot, adds depth to the plot. Their on-screen relationship emphasizes the partnership that served as the foundation for the Clicquot history. The film does not shy away from the difficulties they encountered, depicting the personal and professional hardships that forged Barbe-Nicole's determination.

As the story progresses, the viewer sees Barbe-Nicole grow from a heartbroken widow to a trailblazing entrepreneur. Her strategic initiatives, from overcoming trade embargoes to obtaining worldwide markets, are portrayed with historical accuracy and dramatic flair. The film's tempo keeps spectators engaged, alternating between periods of contemplation and sequences of frantic business conversations and production obstacles.

"Her wines reflect her character; strong, distinctive, and full of life," wrote a contemporary of Barbe-Nicole. This sentiment is mirrored throughout the film, with each bottle of Veuve Clicquot serving as a tribute to her lasting legacy. The story of Widow Clicquot is about more than simply champagne; it's about resilience, inventiveness, and the unbreakable character of a woman who refused to let her circumstances define her.

Barbe-Nicole built Veuve Clicquot into one of the world's most renowned champagne houses in the years after her husband's death. Her influence in the industry is immense. She pioneered processes that are still in use today and established quality and branding standards that continue to impact winemakers. Her legacy lives on not only in the bottles of champagne named after her, but also in the innumerable women who have been inspired by her narrative to chase their own aspirations.

The film "Widow Clicquot" is a reminder of the power of vision and tenacity. It commemorates the life of a woman who, despite all difficulties, carved out a place for herself in a male-dominated society. Barbe-Nicole Ponsardin Clicquot's tale exemplifies what can be accomplished with daring and inventiveness. Her influence endures, not only in the champagne industry, but also in the larger narrative of women's contributions to business and society.

Historical Context

"In wine, there's truth," an ancient phrase asserts, and few lives reflect this notion more perfectly than Barbe-Nicole Ponsardin Clicquot. Understanding the historical context of her tale provides a vivid backdrop for truly appreciating her astounding achievements. The late 18th and early 19th centuries were times of great upheaval and development in Europe, notably in France, where political, social, and economic revolutions altered the landscape. The tale of the Widow Clicquot originated in this vibrant and frequently violent setting.

The French Revolution, which began in 1789, transformed the fabric of French society. The old regime, with its rigid class hierarchies and monarchical control, was overthrown, paving the way for new ideas of liberty, equality, and brotherhood. However, this period of severe political turmoil resulted in instability and violence. The Reign of Terror, which lasted from 1793 to 1794, saw thousands executed and widespread dread, leaving severe scars on the country. Barbe-Nicole was born during this time in Reims, a city in France's Champagne region, to a rich family with roots in the local textile industry. Her upbringing was shaped by the seismic events that occurred around her, making her a tenacious and adaptable person.

The end of the Revolution did not result in quick tranquility. Napoleon Bonaparte's emergence in 1799 signaled a new age of authoritarian authority, but one that incorporated many revolutionary concepts. During Napoleon's reign, France became entangled in the Napoleonic Wars, which lasted from 1803 to 1815. These disputes included numerous European countries and had far-reaching implications for international trade and business. These years proved especially difficult for the Champagne region's developing wine industry. Trade embargoes, blockades, and the constant fear of military conflict made wine exports difficult and risky.

Barbe-Nicole married François Clicquot in 1798, amid war and political instability. François was the son of Philippe Clicquot, a wealthy banker and textile dealer who had lately entered the wine industry. The marriage was more than a personal union; it was a strategic partnership that brought together the riches and ambitions of two powerful families. François was extremely enthusiastic about the possibilities of Champagne wine, and with Barbe-Nicole's help, they proceeded to invest heavily in the business.

The Champagne industry saw a period of experimentation and expansion in the early nineteenth century. The manufacture of sparkling wine was still in its early stages, with many technical obstacles to solve. The méthode champenoise, or sparkling wine method, entailed stimulating a secondary fermentation in the bottle to produce carbonation. This method, while revolutionary, was laden with hazards, including the possibility of bottles bursting owing to pressure buildup. Barbe-Nicole and François dedicated themselves to perfecting this approach, hoping to create a product that would stand out in the competitive wine market.

In 1805, tragedy struck when François died unexpectedly, leaving Barbe-Nicole a widow at the age of 27. Barbe-Nicole made the courageous choice to take charge of the firm herself, at a time when women were expected to withdraw from public life after their spouses died. Her decision was unprecedented and risky. Women in early nineteenth-century France had few legal rights and were virtually excluded from the economic sector. Barbe-Nicole's decision to take on this post was both a personal and professional gamble.

Despite these severe challenges, Barbe-Nicole shown exceptional commercial acumen and tenacity. She understood that innovation was critical to the survival and success of her organization. One of her most major achievements to the Champagne business was the invention of the riddling technique, which she implemented around 1816. This technique entailed placing bottles at an angle and tilting them frequently to accumulate sediment around the cork, which could then be easily removed. This method significantly increased the clarity and flavor of the wine, distinguishing Veuve Clicquot from its competitors.

Barbe-Nicole's efforts to grow her market were also deliberate. She recognized the significance of developing a strong brand identity and created an image of luxury and exclusivity for Veuve Clicquot. She targeted high-end markets throughout Europe, ensuring that her champagne was served at royal courts and renowned occasions. This not only increased demand, but also strengthened the brand's image as a symbol of sophistication and celebration.

In France, the Restoration Era marked a return to more traditional political and social standards following Napoleon's death. The monarchy was reestablished, and there was a widespread desire to restore order and stability following years of unrest and conflict. Barbe-Nicole saw both obstacles and opportunities during this time period. The reversion to traditional values meant that her work as an entrepreneur was still regarded as unorthodox. However, the newfound emphasis on luxury and refinement benefited her, as Veuve Clicquot champagne became a popular indulgence among Europe's elite.
Veuve Clicquot's international reach grew dramatically throughout the 1820s and 1830s. Barbe-Nicole had solid trading relationships with countries throughout Europe,

including Russia, which became one of her most important customers. The Russian nobility acquired a particular liking for her champagne, and no celebration was considered complete without a bottle of Veuve Clicquot. This age of expansion was not without obstacles. The political situation in Europe remained uncertain, and economic changes posed ongoing challenges to international trade.

Despite these hurdles, Barbe-Nicole's strategic vision and unwavering commitment to excellence secured her company's continuous expansion and success. By the time she died in 1866, she had established Veuve Clicquot as a global brand known for its quality and inventiveness. Her role as a Champagne pioneer and a leader for women in business is still acknowledged today.

The historical background of Barbe-Nicole's life emphasizes the remarkable quality of her accomplishments. Her narrative is one of resilience and ingenuity amidst great social and political change. As Europe dealt with the repercussions of revolution and war,

Barbe-Nicole charted a course that defied tradition and revolutionized the opportunities for women in business. Her contributions to the Champagne sector not only transformed production procedures, but also set a standard of excellence that continues to inspire winemakers all over the world. The Widow Clicquot's narrative exemplifies the power of vision, determination, and the timeless attraction of a well-crafted glass of Champagne.

CHAPTER ONE
Plot Summary

In the heart of France's Champagne region, a story emerges that weaves together love, ambition, and resilience against the backdrop of historical upheaval. This is the story of Barbe-Nicole Ponsardin Clicquot, a woman whose life not only transformed the champagne industry, but also questioned conventional standards of the day. The film "Widow Clicquot," based on Tilar J. Mazzeo's book, brings Barbe-Nicole's incredible story to life, capturing the essence of her unwavering spirit and brilliant mind.

Barbe-Nicole was born in 1777, and her early life was impacted by the tumult of the French Revolution. Growing up in Reims, she saw personally the enormous movements in political power and the demise of the old aristocratic system. Her family, who was deeply involved in the local textile industry, managed to weather these shifts, instilling in her a sense of tenacity and adaptation. These characteristics would eventually prove useful as she confronted her own set of obstacles.

Barbe-Nicole married François Clicquot, a wine trader's son, in 1798. Although their marriage was arranged, it rapidly developed into a partnership based on mutual respect and common goals. François, recognizing his wife's sharp intelligence and economic aptitude, including her in the operations of their new champagne enterprise. They had a vision of growing their tiny business into a well-known brand.

Tragically, François died abruptly in 1805, leaving Barbe-Nicole widowed at the age of 27. Barbe-Nicole made the courageous decision to take over the firm at a period when women were expected to stay out of the spotlight. Her willpower was tested right away as she confronted a male-dominated sector, economic insecurity, and the continuing Napoleonic Wars, which disrupted trade lines and presented enormous financial hazards.

Barbe-Nicole's first big difficulty was to perfect the technique of producing sparkling wine. The méthode champenoise, a process that uses a secondary fermentation in the bottle to produce carbonation, was still being improved. The technique was riddled with challenges, including the possibility of bottles bursting owing to pressure buildup. Undeterred, Barbe-Nicole dedicated time and resources to learning this technique. Her tenacity paid off when the riddling procedure was developed about 1816. This technique, which included repeatedly tilting bottles at an angle to collect sediment near the cork for easier removal, substantially increased the clarity and flavor of her champagne.

With a superior product in hand, Barbe-Nicole focused on branding and marketing. She realized that in order to stand out in a crowded market, she needed to develop a unique personality. She picked a bright yellow label, which clearly distinguished her bottles and became a brand signature. This attention to detail extended to her marketing efforts, in which she used the quality of her goods as well as her personal story to appeal to Europe's elite.

Barbe-Nicole's approach to entering international markets was deliberate and tenacious. She concentrated on Russia, a profitable yet tough market due to current political concerns. Her perseverance was rewarded when the Russian nobility developed a strong preference for her champagne. Stories of her champagne being served at Tsar Alexander I's court became part of the brand's legend, adding to its grandeur and desirability. This achievement in Russia marked a watershed moment for Veuve Clicquot, cementing the brand's reputation for luxury and excellence around the world.

Barbe-Nicole endured various personal and professional problems over the course of her career. The political situation in Europe remained turbulent, and economic changes posed ongoing challenges to her firm. However, her strategic vision and adaptability secured Veuve Clicquot's sustained expansion and success. She built a loyal and motivated crew, instilling a sense of family in her organization. This method not only increased productivity, but also provided a solid foundation for her firm.

Barbe-Nicole's influence stretched beyond the Champagne business. Her narrative has become a symbol of female empowerment and enterprise. She defied traditional expectations of women at the time, demonstrating that determination and inventiveness could overcome even the most daunting obstacles. Her legacy has motivated countless women to pursue their goals and break cultural standards.

The film "Widow Clicquot" depicts Barbe-Nicole's journey in astonishing detail and emotional depth. Barbe-Nicole's portrayal by Haley Bennett captures the complexities of her character, including her fragility, strength, and unwavering drive. The film's historical accuracy, paired with its captivating narrative, make it an effective tribute to a lady who altered the path of an industry.

Set against the breathtaking background of the Champagne region, the film's cinematography is a visual feast. The beautiful vines and old cellars provide a fascinating backdrop for Barbe-Nicole's narrative. The vintage costumes and intricate settings transport spectators to a world on the verge of modernization, reflecting the excitement and uncertainty of the time.

The supporting cast, which includes Tom Sturridge as François Clicquot, provides complexity to the story. Their on-screen relationship exemplifies the partnership that established the Clicquot tradition. The film does not shy away from the difficulties they encountered, depicting the personal and professional hardships that forged Barbe-Nicole's determination.

As the story progresses, viewers see Barbe-Nicole grow from a sad widow to a trailblazing entrepreneur. Her strategic initiatives, from overcoming trade embargoes to obtaining worldwide markets, are portrayed with historical accuracy and dramatic flare. The film's tempo keeps spectators engaged, alternating between periods of contemplation and sequences of frantic business conversations and production obstacles.

Each bottle of Veuve Clicquot represents Barbe-Nicole's lasting legacy. Her wines are a reflection of her personality: powerful, distinct, and vibrant. The story of Widow Clicquot is about more than simply champagne; it's about resilience, inventiveness, and the unbreakable character of a woman who refused to let her circumstances define her.

Barbe-Nicole built Veuve Clicquot into one of the world's most renowned champagne houses by the time she died in 1866. Her influence in the industry is immense. She pioneered processes that are still in use today and established quality and branding standards that continue to impact winemakers. Her legacy lives on not only in the bottles of champagne named after her, but also in the innumerable women who have been inspired by her narrative to chase their own aspirations.

The film "Widow Clicquot" is a reminder of the power of vision and tenacity. It commemorates the life of a woman who, despite all difficulties, carved out a place for herself in a male-dominated society. Barbe-Nicole Ponsardin Clicquot's tale exemplifies what can be accomplished with daring and inventiveness. Her influence endures, not only in the champagne industry, but also in the larger narrative of women's contributions to business and society.

Barbe-Nicole's path, from the early challenges after François' death to the achievements of developing a global brand, is a master class in entrepreneurship and leadership. Her capacity to convert hardship into opportunity is a lesson that can be applied across generations. The difficulties she encountered, whether in mastering the complexity of champagne production or managing the complexities of international trade, demonstrate her inventiveness and determination.

The precise artistry required to make Veuve Clicquot champagne reflects Barbe-Nicole's own business strategy. Every stage of the production process, from the careful selection of grapes to the precision of the riddling technique, demonstrates her dedication to perfection. This dedication meant that each bottle bearing the Clicquot name met the greatest standards, garnering the trust and admiration of people all over the world.

Barbe-Nicole's narrative is also a fascinating investigation into human development and empowerment. Her rise from a secluded young woman to a powerful business leader exemplifies the transformational power of self-belief and perseverance. The encouragement she received from her family and the respect she garnered from her peers highlight the value of community and collaboration in accomplishing great things.

The ongoing popularity of Veuve Clicquot champagne is a monument to Barbe-Nicole's heritage. Her breakthroughs in production and marketing laid the groundwork for a brand that thrives decades later. The yellow label, originally a bold marketing strategy, has become an iconic sign of quality and elegance. The values she established—uncompromising quality, smart branding, and a worldwide vision—remain the foundations of the company's success.

Barbe-Nicole's influence extends beyond the realm of wine. Her narrative has encouraged numerous entrepreneurs, particularly women, to pursue their aspirations and overcome the limitations of their times.

Her story is a striking reminder that excellence can emerge from the most difficult conditions. Her legacy, as depicted in the film and book, continues to inspire and uplift, demonstrating that with passion and determination, everything is possible.

The story of Widow Clicquot is a celebration of the human spirit and inventiveness. It's a timeless story that speaks to audiences today just as much as it did in Barbe-Nicole's day. The film captures the essence of her journey with realism and grace, paying tribute to a lady whose influence on the world of champagne—and the world in general—is unrivaled. The story of Barbe-Nicole Ponsardin Clicquot is a source of inspiration, demonstrating the power of vision, resilience, and an unwavering pursuit of greatness.

CHAPTER TWO
Main Characters

"Barbe-Nicole Ponsardin, better known as the Veuve Clicquot, was not merely a widow but a visionary who transformed the champagne industry during an era when women were seldom seen at the helm of businesses."

Barbe-Nicole Ponsardin's journey began in the late 18th century, in Reims, France, where she was born into a wealthy and powerful family. Her father, Ponce Jean Nicolas Philippe Ponsardin, was a prominent businessman who actively supported the French Revolution. Barbe-Nicole grew up in an affluent household and acquired an education uncommon for women at the time. This foundation paved the way for her future undertakings. Barbe-Nicole married François Clicquot, the wealthy winemaking family's son, when she was 20 years old. Their relationship was more than simply a personal bond; it was also a strategic collaboration that would ultimately influence the future of the champagne business. Despite their arranged marriage, they established a deep and emotional relationship together. François, like his father, was passionate about winemaking, and the two went on a mission to grow the family business.

Tragically, François Clicquot died suddenly in 1805, leaving Barbe-Nicole a widow at the age of 27. Barbe-Nicole chose to take over her late husband's business, defying traditional norms at a time when widows were expected to fade away. Many people, including her own family, questioned and opposed her decision. However, she was keen to demonstrate her abilities.

Barbe-Nicole encountered various hurdles as she gained control of the company. The Napoleonic Wars had created an unstable economic climate, with trade blockades having a particular impact on the wine business. Furthermore, previous champagne production processes were labor-intensive and complicated, frequently resulting in variable quality and enormous loss from exploding bottles.

Undeterred, Barbe-Nicole engaged herself in the complexities of winemaking, looking for creative answers to the industry's difficulties. One of her most notable accomplishments was the establishment of the méthode champenoise, a procedure for improving the fermentation and clarification of champagne. This procedure entailed placing the bottles upside down and spinning them frequently to gather sediment in the bottle's neck, which was then removed. This procedure, known as riddling, resulted in a clear and stable product, setting a new benchmark in champagne manufacturing.

Her perseverance paid off, and by 1814, Barbe-Nicole had successfully produced a batch of high-quality champagne. However, the political situation remained turbulent, and Russia's invasion of France presented a new threat to her firm. She took advantage of an opportunity during the confusion and decided to ship her champagne to Russia. This daring action paid off when her product was well-received, giving her a foothold in the profitable Russian market.

Barbe-Nicole and her company experienced a watershed moment when her champagne became popular in Russia. Veuve Clicquot began to achieve international prominence for its superior quality and creative procedures. Barbe-Nicole's image as a savvy and resourceful entrepreneur increased, garnering her the admiration of both peers and competitors.

Barbe-Nicole displayed exceptional adaptability and innovation throughout her career. She developed the first vintage champagne in 1810, distinguishing her brand from competitors and catering to her clients' changing tastes.

Her attention on quality control and branding helped Veuve Clicquot become a symbol of luxury and excellence.

Aside from her contributions to winemaking, Barbe-Nicole was a pioneer for women in business. At a time when female business was virtually unknown, she broke down boundaries and set a precedent for future generations. Her leadership style was defined by tenacity, innovation, and a thorough awareness of the business. She was recognized for her hands-on attitude, often personally overseeing the manufacturing process to ensure that her high standards were met.

Barbe-Nicole's story is also about resilience. Despite countless personal and professional losses, she stayed committed to her mission. Her ability to handle the difficulties of the commercial world, along with her imaginative spirit, enabled her to create an empire that has lasted centuries.

One of Barbe-Nicole's defining events was her work with Edouard Werlé, a young and skilled businessman who joined Veuve Clicquot in the 1820s. Their cooperation was extremely successful, with Werlé playing a critical role in the company's expansion and modernization. Veuve Clicquot continued to grow under their shared direction, establishing itself as one of the world's leading champagne houses.

Barbe-Nicole's effect lasted beyond her lifetime. Her legacy is seen in the continuous success of the Veuve Clicquot brand, which is still a champagne market leader today. The ideas she established—innovation, quality, and a never-ending pursuit of excellence—continue to guide the business.

Barbe-Nicole was given the title "La Grande Dame de la Champagne" in acknowledgment of her contributions, demonstrating her influence in the business. Her life and achievements have inspired countless others, both inside and outside of the wine industry, and her tale is a strong reminder of what can be accomplished with vision, perseverance, and courage.

Barbe-Nicole Ponsardin Clicquot's transformation from a young widow to a trailblazing businesswoman is an inspiring story of perseverance and creativity. Her capacity to overcome hardship and turn problems into opportunities demonstrates her remarkable character and business acumen. Her work not only transformed the champagne industry, but also opened the path for subsequent generations of female business leaders.

Veuve Clicquot's lasting prosperity reflects Barbe-Nicole's legacy. Her tale continues to resonate, inspiring others who dare to dream and strive for perfection. Barbe-Nicole Ponsardin Clicquot continues to be a symbol of tenacity, creativity, and the force of vision, reminding us that even in the face of immense challenges, incredible achievements are achievable.

CHAPTER THREE
Debra May

"To succeed, you have to believe in something with such a passion that it becomes a reality." This comment by Anita Roddick, the founder of The Body Shop, captures the energy and determination of Barbe-Nicole Ponsardin Clicquot, aka the Widow Clicquot. Her story is not just one of personal success, but also a thorough examination of numerous topics and patterns that strike a chord with both   readers   and   viewers.

"Innovation" is a key theme in Widow Clicquot's narrative. At a time when the champagne business was plagued by inefficiencies and inconsistencies, Barbe-Nicole's unwavering pursuit of betterment resulted in ground-breaking advances. Her invention of the méthode champenoise revolutionized champagne production, ensuring clarity and stability in every bottle. This idea was formed out of necessity, not luxury. Faced with severe

hurdles, such as economic instability and the prospect of bankruptcy, Barbe-Nicole's inventive spirit demonstrated her resilience and ingenuity. She simplified the riddling procedure, which involves periodically turning bottles to collect sediment in the neck, and it became the industry standard. This subject of innovation emphasizes the need of thinking outside the box and constantly striving for progress, especially in the face of overwhelming challenges.

Barbe-Nicole's life is also marked by a strong sense of resilience. Widowed at the age of 27 and left with a floundering business, she could have easily succumbed to societal pressures and expectations. Instead, she decided to fight. Her journey was laden with difficulties, from the Napoleonic Wars, which hindered trade, to the mistrust she encountered as a woman running a business in the early nineteenth century. Nonetheless, Barbe-Nicole's tenacity shone through. She showed unflinching dedication to her goal, working relentlessly to secure the success of her champagne. This perseverance was not just about overcoming adversity, but also about adapting to changing circumstances and discovering new paths to achievement. Her ability to traverse these problems serves as a strong reminder of the fortitude and determination required to face life's challenges.

The notion of *"empowerment"* is also interwoven throughout Barbe-Nicole's story. In an era when women were underrepresented in senior positions, she broke down barriers and established new precedents. Her accomplishment was more than simply a personal victory; it was also a big step forward for women in business. Barbe-Nicole's leadership style, which included hands-on involvement and a thorough understanding of her sector, won her respect and appreciation. She became a role model for future generations of female entrepreneurs, demonstrating that gender is not a barrier to success. This subject of empowerment emphasizes the significance of questioning cultural conventions and working for more inclusion and equality in all aspects of life.

Another important theme in Widow Clicquot's story is *"legacy"*. Barbe-Nicole's influence on the champagne industry lasts much beyond her lifetime. The ideas she established—innovation, quality, and excellence—still guide the Veuve Clicquot brand today. Her story demonstrates how one person may have a long-term impact on a whole industry. The legacy motif highlights the value of creating something that will last, leaving a positive and enduring impression on future generations. Barbe-Nicole's life is a compelling example of how one person's vision and dedication may change the course of history.

Barbe-Nicole Ponsardin Clicquot's life is also marked by a strong emphasis on adaptation. Throughout her career, she has experienced several shifts and difficulties, ranging from political upheavals to economic catastrophes. Her capacity to adjust to shifting conditions was critical to her success. When the Napoleonic Wars threatened her business, she sought new markets for her champagne. When traditional methods of production proved inefficient, she created new techniques. This adaptability emphasizes the significance of being adaptable and receptive to changing circumstances, a lesson that is just as applicable today as it was in Barbe-Nicole's time.

The concept of *"vision"* is important to Barbe-Nicole's story. Her capacity to look beyond the present problems and imagine a prosperous future for her company was a motivating force behind her accomplishments. She had a clear vision of what she wanted to accomplish and stayed focused on it, even when the way seemed unclear. This vision, paired with her innovative spirit and resilience, helped her transform a faltering company into a global brand. The theme of vision emphasizes the significance of having a strong sense of direction and purpose in achieving success.

"Passion" is another recurring topic in Barbe-Nicole's life. Her deep love of winemaking and dedication to producing high-quality champagne were clear in everything she did. This passion motivated her perseverance and invention, propelling her to overcome challenges and push the limits of what was possible. The theme of passion emphasizes the importance of discovering and pursuing your passions,

as they can provide the drive and energy required to achieve great things.

Barbe-Nicole's narrative also delves into the issue of *"risk-taking"* Her decision to take over the family business after her husband's death, as well as her decision to ship champagne to Russia during the Napoleonic Wars, involved major risk. These daring acts were critical to her success, highlighting the value of taking calculated risks in order to reap large returns. The risk-taking motif emphasizes the need of pushing outside one's comfort zone and being willing to embrace uncertainty in the pursuit of achievement.

"Determination" is a motif that is closely linked to Barbe-Nicole's path. Her resolve to succeed, despite the multiple hurdles she faced, was important in her success. She refused to give up, even though the odds were stacked against her. This tenacity was demonstrated by her unwavering pursuit of excellence and innovation, as well as her capacity to overcome setbacks and keep moving forward. The theme of determination emphasizes the value

of perseverance and tenacity in accomplishing one's goals.

"Transformation" is an essential theme in Widow Clicquot's narrative. Barbe-Nicole altered not only her firm, but the champagne industry as a whole. Her inventive skills and dedication to quality created new norms, transforming champagne from a local product to a worldwide luxury brand. This transformational topic emphasizes the ability of vision and innovation to effect substantial change and open up new opportunities.

The narrative of Barbe-Nicole Ponsardin Clicquot also exemplifies the topic of *"leadership"*. Her ability to guide her company through difficult times, encourage her employees, and make strategic judgments was critical to her success. She proved that good leadership entails not only managing day-to-day operations, but also creating a clear vision for the future and pushing others to strive toward it. The leadership theme focuses on the abilities and skills required to guide a business or organization to success.

"Courage" is a motif that runs throughout Barbe-Nicole's tale. It required enormous fortitude to take over the family firm at such a young age and in a male-dominated profession. Her willingness to conduct bold activities, such as delivering champagne to Russia during a war, demonstrates her fearlessness. The theme of courage emphasizes the need of being courageous and daring in pursuing one's goals, even when confronted with substantial dangers and obstacles.

"Perseverance" is another important topic in the story of Widow Clicquot. Barbe-Nicole faced countless challenges and failures along the way, but she stayed determined to succeed. Her determination helped her overcome these obstacles and attain her ambitions. This subject emphasizes the necessity of sticking to one's vision and pushing forward in the face of hardship.

"Excellence" is a motif that runs throughout Barbe-Nicole's life and career. Her dedication to making high-quality champagne was the driving cause behind her success. She set high standards for herself and her firm,

and her quest of excellence contributed to Veuve Clicquot's status as an industry leader. The concept of excellence emphasizes the value of aiming for the best in all one does.

"Legacy" is a reoccurring theme throughout Barbe-Nicole's tale. Her contributions to the champagne industry, as well as her role as a pioneer for women in business, have left a lasting legacy that continues to inspire and influence others. Her narrative serves as a reminder of the long-term impact that one person's vision, determination, and creativity can have in the world.

The story of Widow Clicquot also explores the concept of **independence**. Barbe-Nicole was able to escape and live a rather comfortable life when her husband died. Instead, she decided to establish her independence and take charge of her fate. Her decision to run the company on her own terms was a brave and courageous move that demonstrated her desire for autonomy and self-determination. The subject of independence emphasizes the necessity of taking control of one's life and making decisions that are consistent with one's values and aspirations.

Barbe-Nicole Ponsardin Clicquot's story is around entrepreneurship. Her journey from young widow to successful businesswoman demonstrates her entrepreneurial spirit. She saw opportunities, took cautious risks, and worked relentlessly to establish and expand her firm. The entrepreneurship theme emphasizes the value of invention, resilience, and strategic thinking in establishing a successful business.

"Pioneering spirit" is another characteristic that characterizes Barbe-Nicole's life. She was a trailblazer in many ways, breaking new ground in the champagne industry and establishing new standards for quality and production. Her pioneering spirit was evident in her desire to test new approaches and her determination to achieve in a male-dominated field. This subject emphasizes the value of being willing to explore new frontiers and push the limits of what is possible.

Barbe-Nicole's work is characterized by a consistent

emphasis on quality. Her dedication to produce the greatest quality champagne was important in her success. She recognized that maintaining high standards was critical to establishing a strong and recognizable brand. The theme of quality highlights the necessity of attention to details.

CHAPTER FOUR

The Arrest and Execution

Barbe-Nicole Ponsardin Clicquot's tale is one of incredible invention, resilience, and empowerment. These themes and motifs pervade her journey and highlight the story of her life, providing unique insights into her character and the impact she had on the champagne business.

Barbe-Nicole, also known as the Widow Clicquot, was thrown into an unexpected role after her husband, François Clicquot, died in 1805. Widowed at 27, she had to make a difficult decision: sell the family firm or take over and shepherd it through uncertain times. This decision was a bold demonstration of her tenacity. In an era when traditional standards confined women to the background, particularly in business, Barbe-Nicole took the unconventional route. Her choice demonstrated her inner strength and drive.

Barbe-Nicole faced enormous hurdles. The Napoleonic Wars created a turbulent economic climate, disrupting trade channels and causing market turbulence. Despite these challenges, she remained undeterred. Her inventive energy shone through as she worked to modify traditional champagne production procedures. Champagne production was notoriously inconsistent at the period, with many bottles exploding owing to pressure errors. Barbe-Nicole's tireless pursuit of perfection resulted in the creation of the méthode champenoise, a technique for refining the fermentation and clarifying processes. This process ensured that the sediment was collected in the bottle's neck, where it could subsequently be removed, yielding a clearer and more stable product. This innovation not only established a new industry standard, but it also greatly decreased waste, increasing the profitability and prestige of Veuve Clicquot champagne.

Barbe-Nicole's tale is also one of empowerment. Taking over the family company in the early nineteenth century, when women's duties were mostly limited to the domestic sphere, she broke down barriers and redefined what women might accomplish. Her leadership approach was hands-on; she was recognized for personally overseeing manufacturing processes and ensuring that the highest quality standards were met. Her business success and the respect she earned from her coworkers and competition were important accomplishments in a male-dominated age. Her experience motivated many women to follow their goals, defying cultural standards that attempted to confine them.

The idea of legacy is central to Barbe-Nicole's existence. Her contributions to the champagne industry have lasted even after her death. The ideas she created, such as a devotion to quality and innovation, still guide the Veuve Clicquot brand today. Her legacy is reflected not just in the bottles of champagne bearing her name, but also in the corporate processes and standards she established. This enduring impact emphasizes the necessity of developing something that will have a good and long-term impact on future   generations.

Barbe-Nicole's leadership style was also distinguished by her adaptability. She endured several hurdles, including political upheavals and economic downturns, yet she consistently found ways to adapt and succeed. When war interrupted established markets, she looked abroad for fresh chances. Her choice to export champagne to Russia during the Napoleonic blockades was audacious and hazardous, but it ultimately paid off, gaining a new market and elevating the brand's status. This adaptability emphasizes the significance of being flexible and adaptable to changing conditions, a lesson that is still applicable in today's fast-paced business climate.

Barbe-Nicole's visionary approach was a key factor in her success. She had a clear vision of what she wanted to accomplish and stayed focused on it, even when the path was challenging. Her capacity to look beyond the present obstacles and imagine a prosperous future for her company was a motivating force behind her success. This vision, paired with her innovative spirit and resilience, helped her transform a faltering company into a global brand.

Passion is another recurring topic in Barbe-Nicole's life. Her deep love of winemaking and dedication to producing high-quality champagne were clear in everything she did. This passion motivated her perseverance and invention, propelling her to overcome challenges and push the limits of what was possible. The theme of passion emphasizes the importance of discovering and pursuing your passions, as they can provide the drive and energy required to achieve   great   things.

Barbe-Nicole's story also delves into the issue of risk-taking. Her decision to take over the family business after her husband's death, as well as her decision to ship champagne to Russia during the Napoleonic Wars, involved major risk. These daring acts were critical to her success, highlighting the value of taking calculated risks in order to reap large returns. The risk-taking motif emphasizes the need of pushing outside one's comfort zone and being willing to embrace uncertainty in the pursuit of achievement.

Determination is a motif that runs throughout Barbe-Nicole's path. Her resolve to succeed, despite the multiple hurdles she faced, was important in her success. She refused to give up, even though the odds were stacked against her. This tenacity was demonstrated by her unwavering pursuit of excellence and innovation, as well as her capacity to overcome setbacks and keep moving forward.

Widow Clicquot's story also includes a strong emphasis on transformation. Barbe-Nicole altered not only her firm, but the champagne industry as a whole. Her inventive skills and dedication to quality created new norms, transforming champagne from a local product to a worldwide luxury brand. This transformational topic emphasizes the ability of vision and innovation to effect substantial change and open up new opportunities.

The narrative of Barbe-Nicole Ponsardin Clicquot exemplifies the topic of leadership. Her ability to guide her company through difficult times, encourage her employees, and make strategic judgments was critical to her success. She exemplified the attributes of a great leader, including resilience, vision, and the capacity to inspire and encourage people. The theme of leadership focuses on the qualities and talents required to guide a business or organization to success.

Courage is a significant theme in Barbe-Nicole's tale. It required enormous fortitude to take over the family firm at such a young age and in a male-dominated profession. Her willingness to conduct bold activities, such as delivering champagne to Russia during a war, demonstrates her fearlessness. The theme of courage emphasizes the need of being courageous and daring in pursuing one's goals, even when confronted with substantial dangers and obstacles.

Perseverance is another important motif in the story of Widow Clicquot. Barbe-Nicole faced countless challenges and failures along the way, but she stayed determined to succeed. Her determination helped her overcome these obstacles and attain her ambitions. This subject emphasizes the necessity of sticking to one's vision and pushing forward in the face of hardship.

Barbe-Nicole's life and work are characterized by a commitment to excellence. Her dedication to making high-quality champagne was the driving cause behind her success. She set high standards for herself and her firm, and her quest of excellence contributed to Veuve Clicquot's status as an industry leader. The concept of excellence emphasizes the value of aiming for the best in all one does.

Legacy is a reoccurring theme in Barbe-Nicole's tale. Her contributions to the champagne industry, as well as her role as a pioneer for women in business, have left a lasting legacy that continues to inspire and influence others. Her narrative serves as a reminder of the long-term impact that one person's vision, determination, and creativity can have in the world.

Independence is another major aspect in Barbe-Nicole's story. Barbe-Nicole was able to escape and live a rather comfortable life when her husband died. Instead, she decided to establish her independence and take charge of her fate. Her decision to run the company on her own terms was a brave and courageous move that demonstrated her desire for autonomy and self-determination.

Barbe-Nicole Ponsardin Clicquot's story centers around entrepreneurship. Her journey from young widow to successful businesswoman demonstrates her entrepreneurial spirit. She saw opportunities, took cautious risks, and worked relentlessly to establish and expand her firm. The entrepreneurship theme emphasizes the value of invention, resilience, and strategic thinking in establishing a successful business.

Barbe-Nicole's life is also defined by her pioneering attitude. She was a trailblazer in many ways, breaking new ground in the champagne industry and establishing new standards for quality and production. Her pioneering spirit was evident in her desire to test new approaches and her determination to achieve in a male-dominated field. This subject emphasizes the value of being willing to explore new frontiers and push the limits of what is possible.

Barbe-Nicole Ponsardin Clicquot's life is a multifaceted tapestry of themes and patterns that provide excellent lessons and insights. Her narrative of invention, resilience, and empowerment continues to inspire and resonate, reminding us of the strength of vision, drive, and the human spirit in overcoming difficulties and achieving greatness.

CHAPTER FIVE
Historical Accuracy

The story of Barbe-Nicole Ponsardin Clicquot, the Widow

Clicquot, is a gripping tale that weaves together historical events, societal norms, and personal determination. The historical authenticity of this story is critical to understanding her genuine impact on the champagne industry and her role as a trailblazing businesswoman in the early nineteenth century.

Barbe-Nicole was born in Reims, France, in 1777, during a period of significant change. The French Revolution, which began in 1789, upended the country's social and economic structures. Her father, Ponce Jean Nicolas Philippe Ponsardin, was a prominent textile businessman and a strong backer of the revolution, putting the family in jeopardy during the chaotic years that followed. This experience gave Barbe-Nicole a unique viewpoint on perseverance and adaptation, which would eventually define her entrepreneurial trajectory.

Barbe-Nicole married François Clicquot in 1798, the scion of a well-known winemaking family. Their marriage was more than just the union of two people; it was a strategic alliance that merged their families' money and power. François envisioned extending the family business, particularly in champagne manufacturing, which was still a thriving industry at the time. However, François's sudden death in 1805 left Barbe-Nicole a 27-year-old widow with a small daughter and a faltering business. This was the start of her incredible journey as the Widow Clicquot.

The Napoleonic Wars, which lasted from 1803 to 1815, had a significant impact on the European economy and trade. The continental blockade enforced by Napoleon severely limited trade channels, making it difficult for firms to function. Despite these obstacles, Barbe-Nicole shown extraordinary resourcefulness. She took over the company, a risky decision at a period when women were never active in business. Her decision to concentrate on enhancing the quality and production of champagne was a calculated risk that paid off.

Barbe-Nicole made one of the most significant contributions to the champagne business by developing the méthode champenoise, often known as the classic method. Prior to this breakthrough, champagne production was erratic, with many bottles exploding as a result of pressure buildup from secondary fermentation. The méthode champenoise entailed a number of procedures, including riddling (remuage) and disgorgement (dégorgement), which helped clarify the wine and maintain uniformity. Barbe-Nicole's commitment to improving this technology was crucial in making champagne a luxury product. Her careful dedication to quality control, combined with her inventive methodologies, established new industry standards.

The historical backdrop of Barbe-Nicole's success is critical to evaluating her accomplishments. The early nineteenth century saw substantial social and economic development in Europe. The Industrial Revolution was gaining traction, resulting in changes in production methods and trading habits. However, women's roles in business have remained limited. Barbe-Nicole's ability to break down these boundaries and establish herself as a key player in the champagne industry demonstrates her incredible vision and determination.

Barbe-Nicole's success was partly affected by her strategic marketing decisions. After Napoleon's defeat in 1814, she recognized a chance to enter the Russian market, which had a growing desire for luxury products. Despite the risks, she sent a large quantity of her champagne to Russia. The operation was a huge success, strengthening Veuve Clicquot's brand in one of the most profitable markets at the time. This decision demonstrates her forethought and willingness to take measured risks, both of which are crucial characteristics for any successful entrepreneur.

The historical truth of Barbe-Nicole's story is supported by a variety of sources that describe her life and achievements. Tilar J. Mazzeo's biography, "The Widow Clicquot: The Story of a Champagne Empire and the Woman Who Ruled It," offers a detailed narrative of her life, backed up by significant research and historical sources. Mazzeo's work emphasizes Barbe-Nicole's discoveries, problems, and impact on the champagne business. Similarly, Gérard Liger-Belair's "Uncorked: The Science of Champagne" delves into the technical aspects of champagne production and the pioneering procedures pioneered by Barbe-Nicole.

Furthermore, Barbe-Nicole's legacy may be seen in the continuous success of the Veuve Clicquot brand. The principles she established—quality, creativity, and perseverance—are still vital to the brand's identity. The brand continues to recognize her contributions through programs such as the Veuve Clicquot Business Woman Award, which honors entrepreneurial women who exemplify Barbe-Nicole's passion.

Understanding the historical authenticity of Barbe-Nicole's account requires considering the broader environment of the wine industry at the time. Champagne, as we know it now, was still in its infancy in the early 1800s. The Champagne region in northeastern France had been producing still wines for generations, but sparkling wines were relatively new. The method of manufacturing sparkling wine presented numerous obstacles, including managing the fermentation process and ensuring the wine's clarity. Barbe-Nicole's improvements in riddling and disgorgement were critical in overcoming these obstacles and paving the way for champagne's global success.

Furthermore, the social and cultural background of the time heavily influenced Barbe-Nicole's journey. The early nineteenth century was defined by tight gender norms and expectations. Women were often expected to focus on home chores, and those who moved into business faced strong hostility. Barbe-Nicole's victory was both a personal triumph and a challenge to society conventions. Her ability to traverse the male-dominated world of business while earning the respect of her peers demonstrates her great leadership and tenacity.

Barbe-Nicole's narrative also touches on key historical events and people. Her business thrived throughout France's Restoration period, which was characterized by political and social upheaval following Napoleon's demise. Her capacity to adapt to changing conditions and embrace new chances is a critical component of her success. Furthermore, her relationships with significant persons of the time, notably Russian aristocrats, demonstrate her company's global reach and significance.

Barbe-Nicole's narrative is reinforced by contemporary testimonies and archives, which add to its historical veracity. Letters, business records, and other historical artifacts offer a complete account of her life and activities. These sources demonstrate her rigorous approach to business, inventive spirit, and constant devotion to quality. They also highlight the obstacles she encountered, such as legal disputes, financial difficulties, and the continual danger of competition. Despite these hurdles, Barbe-Nicole remained committed to her vision and continued to push the limits of what was possible.

When determining the historical veracity of Barbe-Nicole's story, it is also necessary to assess the impact of her innovations on the larger wine industry. She perfected the méthode champenoise, which is still used today to produce high-quality sparkling wine. Her approaches have been adopted and modified by winemakers all across the world, demonstrating her lasting impact on the industry. Furthermore, her dedication to quality and concentration on branding and marketing set new industry standards, establishing champagne as a symbol of luxury and celebration.

Barbe-Nicole's legacy can also be seen in the continuous success and renown of the Veuve Clicquot brand. Today, the brand is synonymous with excellence and innovation, embodying the ideals and ideas she founded. The company's dedication to honoring her legacy is shown in its continued efforts to encourage and recognize women in business, such as the Veuve Clicquot Business Woman Award. This award acknowledges and honors entrepreneurial women who represent Barbe-Nicole's enthusiasm and determination, ensuring that her legacy continues to inspire and impact future generations.

Finally, Barbe-Nicole Ponsardin Clicquot, often known as the Widow Clicquot, tells a fascinating story of ingenuity, resilience, and empowerment. Her narrative's historical correctness is well-documented, with sources ranging from biographies to contemporary accounts and archival information. Her contributions to the champagne business, particularly the establishment of the méthode champenoise, established new benchmarks and developed champagne into a global luxury product. Her ability to overcome tremendous obstacles and establish herself as a prominent figure in a male-dominated business demonstrates her outstanding vision and determination. Barbe-Nicole's legacy continues to inspire and influence others, demonstrating the lasting impact of her life and work.

CHAPTER SIX
Production Details

To bring Barbe-Nicole Ponsardin Clicquot's life to the cinema, the film "Widow Clicquot" was produced with rigorous regard to historical detail, imaginative storytelling, and worldwide collaboration. The project began with a thorough examination of the historical setting of early nineteenth-century France, focusing on the turbulent time of the Napoleonic Wars and the ensuing Restoration era. This backdrop was critical for effectively portraying Barbe-Nicole's effort to revolutionize the champagne business.

Erin Dignam and Christopher Monger wrote the screenplay, which was based on Tilar J. Mazzeo's meticulously researched biography "The Widow Clicquot". This biography presented a solid basis of historical facts, personal experiences, and corporate breakthroughs that helped shape Barbe-Nicole's legacy. Dignam and Monger attempted to strike a balance between factual accuracy and appealing narrative elements, ensuring that the video was both educational and entertaining.

Casting was a significant part of the production. Barbe-Nicole Ponsardin Clicquot was played by Haley Bennett, who portrayed the character's strength as well as her sensitivity. Bennett's portrayal was complemented by Tom Sturridge as Barbe-Nicole's husband, François Clicquot.

Their on-screen chemistry and nuanced performances were crucial in expressing the nuances of their relationship and the ensuing difficulties Barbe-Nicole endured following François' tragic death.

Thomas Napper, recognized for his attention to detail and ability to handle historical dramas, was brought on board to lead the production. Napper's goal for the film was to create an immersive experience that took the viewer to the early 1800s, allowing them to see the history of the champagne business via Barbe-Nicole's perspective. His direction emphasized the character's endurance, ingenuity, and determination, ensuring that her story will appeal to modern audiences.

The majority of the film was made in France, with significant scenes shot at Reims and Chablis, both of which are known for producing champagne. The selection of these places was critical to keeping the film's authenticity. The vineyards, old cellars, and châteaux created a lovely and historically authentic setting for the drama. Filming in these places also allowed the cast and crew to capture the essence of the champagne-making process, from grape picking to Barbe-Nicole's innovative riddling and disgorgement processes.

The film's production design, supervised by a team of professional set designers and historical consultants, recreated the period with meticulous realism. From the Clicquot family mansion to the bustling markets of Reims, each set was meticulously designed to replicate the architectural styles and cultural nuances of the time. The smallest elements were carefully considered, including period-appropriate clothing, props, and even the types of tools used in champagne manufacturing. This attention to accuracy extended to the representation of the Napoleonic Wars' influence on the region, which highlighted the economic and social changes that Barbe-Nicole had to deal with.

A team of period fashion experts oversaw the costume design, which played an important role in bringing the characters to life. The outfits were not only historically correct, but also reflected the characters' personalities and social standing. Barbe-Nicole's attire, for example, changed throughout the film to reflect her transition from young widow to successful businesswoman. The materials, colors, and designs were carefully picked to emphasize her tenacity and growing power in the male-dominated world of   business.

The film's cinematography, guided by a skilled director of photography, caught the beauty and drama of the French countryside, as well as Barbe-Nicole's personal moments. The use of natural light and sweeping camera movements contributed to a visually spectacular portrayal of the vineyards and cellars crucial to her story. Close-up images of the champagne-making process added an educational component, allowing viewers to appreciate the craftsmanship needed in manufacturing each bottle.

Music was vital to the film's emotional and narrative arcs. The score, written by an acclaimed composer with experience in historical plays, used classical and contemporary elements to produce a soundscape that emphasized the film's themes of tenacity and creativity. The music was deliberately timed to enhance significant scenes in the plot, ranging from Barbe-Nicole's emotional troubles to her professional successes.

Post-production included significant editing to ensure that the film's rhythm and storytelling were compelling and consistent. The editors collaborated closely with the filmmaker to strike a balance between historical information and emotional tension, ensuring that the film followed a captivating narrative flow. Special effects were employed sparingly yet well to portray historical events, such as the Napoleonic Wars, without taking away from the story's human themes.

Marketing for "Widow Clicquot" emphasized both historical accuracy and modern relevance. Trailers and promotional materials highlighted the film's rich historical backdrop, Barbe-Nicole's inspirational story, and outstanding production qualities. Interviews with the actors and crew, as well as behind-the-scenes material, were used to pique interest and provide insight into the production of the picture. The marketing effort also used social media and digital platforms to reach a global audience, highlighting the film's universal themes of persistence and creativity.

The film premiered at the Toronto International Film Festival and got great feedback for its historical authenticity, strong acting, and captivating plot. Critics complimented Haley Bennett's portrayal of Barbe-Nicole, particularly her ability to express the character's complexity and drive. The film's painstaking attention to detail and realistic portrayal of early nineteenth-century France were also warmly praised.

"Widow Clicquot" is not only a monument to Barbe-Nicole Ponsardin Clicquot, but also an educational tool that illuminates an important chapter in the history of champagne. The film's production aspects, from real locales and costumes to creative storytelling approaches, ensuring that it continues to make an important contribution to cinematic and historical narratives. By bringing Barbe-Nicole's tale to life with such care and accuracy, the filmmakers have left a lasting legacy that recognizes her contributions to the wine and business worlds.

CHAPTER SEVEN
Release and Reception

The release and reception of the film "Widow Clicquot" tell a story that weaves together historical accuracy, cinematic artistry, and public perception. This video, based on Tilar J. Mazzeo's book "The Widow Clicquot: The Story of a Champagne Empire and the Woman Who Ruled

It," tells the story of Barbe-Nicole Ponsardin Clicquot, a trailblazing woman who transformed the champagne business in the early 1800s. The film, directed by Thomas Napper and starring Haley Bennett, has its international premiere at the Toronto International Film Festival (TIFF) on September 11, 2023.

The choice of TIFF for the premiere was a smart decision. TIFF is known for presenting films that combine commercial appeal and artistic creativity, making it a perfect venue for "Widow Clicquot." The film's premiere was widely anticipated, considering the fascinating historical character at its heart and the meticulous adaptation of Mazzeo's celebrated biography. The festival circuit was abuzz with anticipation as the film promised a mix of historical drama, personal triumph, and entrepreneurial spirit, capturing the heart of Barbe-Nicole's amazing   existence.

Critics at TIFF applauded the film's painstaking attention to historical detail and fascinating narrative. Haley Bennett's portrayal of Barbe-Nicole was praised for its depth and sincerity, reflecting the nuances of a woman negotiating the complexity of business and societal demands at a turbulent time in European history. Bennett's portrayal was praised as a tour de force, capturing the Widow Clicquot's perseverance, resilience, and innovative spirit. The supporting cast, which included Tom Sturridge as François Clicquot and Sam Riley as Edouard Werlé, delivered great performances that expanded the story and underlined Barbe-Nicole's combined efforts to success.

Thomas Napper's direction was highly praised for its blend of historical accuracy and cinematic storytelling. The film's visual aesthetic, shot on location in Champagne, France, offered authenticity and a feeling of place, transporting viewers to the vineyards and cellars where Barbe-Nicole's inventions took root. The rich photography, along with a period-appropriate tune, provided an immersive experience that transported viewers to the realm of early nineteenth-century France.

Following its premiere at TIFF, "Widow Clicquot" obtained distribution rights with Vertical Entertainment, ensuring a broad release beginning July 19, 2024. The distribution plan was aimed to capitalize on the film's festival hype as well as the growing interest in stories about historical pioneering women. Marketing efforts stressed the film's historical significance as well as the inspiring story of a lady who overcame adversity to develop a champagne empire.

As the picture gained a larger audience, the reception remained mainly positive. Critics and spectators alike praised the film's combination of historical drama and character-driven storytelling. Rotten Tomatoes recorded an 85% acceptance rating from critics, with many praising the film's captivating portrayal of Barbe-Nicole and thorough attention to detail. Metacritic, which averages reviews from notable publications, gave the picture a 67 out of 100 rating, indicating generally positive reviews.

Audience reactions echoed critical accolades, with spectators praising the film's inspirational story and Bennett's outstanding performance. The film's portrayal of Barbe-Nicole's entrepreneurial journey sparked debate on social media, as did its relevance to current conversations regarding women in business. Many viewers found encouragement in Barbe-Nicole's narrative, noting parallels between her problems and those of today's entrepreneurs.

In-depth reviews from major magazines offered a nuanced analysis on the film's impact. The New York Times lauded the video for shedding light on a little-known historical figure who made groundbreaking contributions to the champagne business. Bennett's performance was described as "captivating and powerful," with the reviewer praising her ability to depict the complexities of a woman managing personal sorrow and professional ambition. The Guardian's review praised the film's visual appeal and ability to bring the historical period to life, calling it "a feast for the eyes and mind."

Christian Zilko of IndieWire had a more negative assessment, stating that while the film succeeded in historical accuracy and performance, it occasionally lapsed into biographical drama clichés. Zilko praised the film's non-linear narrative structure, but noted that several portions of the plot were oversimplified to suit the traditional mold of a "rags-to-riches" story. Despite these criticisms, Zilko recognized the film's overall effectiveness in honoring Barbe-Nicole's accomplishments and contributing to the historical biopic genre.

The film's effect went beyond the box receipts and critical reviews. It reignited interest in Barbe-Nicole Ponsardin Clicquot's life and contributions to the Champagne business. Educational institutions and corporate groups utilized the film as a case study to discuss subjects like creativity, entrepreneurship, and women in leadership. Panels and discussions with historians, business professionals, and the film's creators provided more insight into Barbe-Nicole's legacy and the historical context of her accomplishments.

In France, notably in the Champagne area, the film was lauded as a tribute to a local legend. Barbe-Nicole's hometown and workplace, Reims and Épernay, hosted special screenings and activities. These activities not only celebrated her history, but also demonstrated the ongoing significance of her inventions in the current champagne industry. The video functioned as a cultural touchstone, bringing communities together to honor their ancestry and the lasting legacy of Barbe-Nicole's work.

The film's release had a significant impact on the Veuve Clicquot brand. The corporation used the film's success to highlight its long history and dedication to quality and innovation. Marketing campaigns linked Barbe-Nicole's pioneering attitude to the brand's current objectives, reinforcing the message that the values she founded still guide the company. This convergence of brand messaging with the film's plot strengthened Veuve Clicquot's status as a premium champagne market leader.

In conclusion, the release and reception of "Widow Clicquot" demonstrate a successful combination of historical storytelling, cinematic craftsmanship, and audience participation. The film depicted Barbe-Nicole Ponsardin Clicquot's incredible journey, highlighting her as a trailblazing entrepreneur who bucked cultural standards and transformed the champagne industry. The film not only entertained but also informed and inspired audiences because to its rigorous attention to historical accuracy, captivating acting, and savvy marketing. It emphasized the Widow Clicquot's ongoing legacy and established her status as one of the great business pioneers.

CHAPTER EIGHT
Conclusion

As we reflect on the life and legacy of Barbe-Nicole Ponsardin Clicquot, also known as the Widow Clicquot, it is clear that her narrative is one of amazing resilience, inventiveness, and empowerment. Her rise from young widow to pioneering force in the champagne industry demonstrates her amazing vision and determination. The Widow Clicquot's impact goes long beyond her lifetime, leaving an enduring mark on both the commercial sector and the cultural landscape.

Barbe-Nicole was thrown into an unexpected role after her husband, François Clicquot, died suddenly in 1805. With a small daughter and a floundering wine business, she was confronted with a difficult decision. In an era when women were rarely seen in leadership positions, Barbe-Nicole's choice to take over the family business was nothing short of revolutionary. Her tale exemplifies how adversity may drive great success.

One of the most important components of Barbe-Nicole's legacy is her revolutionary approach to champagne production. The champagne industry in the early 19th century faced numerous obstacles, including uneven quality and severe production inefficiencies. Barbe-Nicole's tireless pursuit of perfection resulted in the creation of the méthode champenoise, a technology that transformed the manufacturing process. This method, which entailed a thorough process of riddling and disgorgement, ensured that the finished product was clear and consistent. Her inventions not only enhanced champagne quality, but also established new industry standards.

Barbe-Nicole's dedication to excellence went beyond the production process. She grasped the value of branding and marketing, realizing that the perception of luxury was critical to the success of her product. Her distinctive yellow label became a sign of excellence, and Veuve

Clicquot swiftly established a reputation for producing some of the world's finest champagne. This emphasis on quality and branding assisted in elevating champagne from a local product to a global symbol of celebration and luxury.

The historical context of Barbe-Nicole's accomplishments is critical to comprehending her significance. The early nineteenth century saw substantial social and economic transformation in Europe. The Napoleonic Wars interrupted conventional trade lines, posing challenges for enterprises throughout the continent. Despite these challenges, Barbe-Nicole showed extraordinary resourcefulness and adaptability. Her choice to transport champagne to Russia during the continental blockade was a risky move that paid off handsomely, securing a rich market and elevating the brand's reputation. This capacity to seize chances amidst upheaval demonstrates her strategic intelligence and vision.

Barbe-Nicole's narrative is also about empowerment. In an era when women's roles were mostly limited to the home, she defied traditional expectations and established herself as a competent business leader. Her victory was more than just a personal triumph; it was also a challenge to the rigid gender conventions of the day. Barbe-Nicole set an example for future generations of female entrepreneurs by taking control of her fate and propelling her company to unparalleled heights. Her tale continues to inspire and motivate women all across the world, proving that determination and vision can overcome even the most severe challenges.

The Veuve Clicquot brand's sustained success and prominence reflect Barbe-Nicole's heritage. The principles she established—innovation, excellence, and perseverance—are still vital to the brand's identity. Today, Veuve Clicquot is synonymous with luxury and perfection, reflecting the principles and standards established by its founder. The company's ongoing initiatives to memorialize her legacy, such as the Veuve Clicquot Business Woman Award, recognize enterprising women who exemplify her energy and determination. This prize not only celebrates remarkable accomplishments, but it also ensures that

Barbe-Nicole's story will continue to inspire future generations.

When assessing Barbe-Nicole's legacy, it is critical to evaluate the larger cultural and historical context of her accomplishments. The rise of the Industrial Revolution, as well as following changes in manufacturing methods and trading procedures, characterized the early nineteenth century. Barbe-Nicole's capacity to adapt to changing circumstances and capitalize on new chances was critical to her success. Her champagne production advancements and smart market expansions contributed significantly to champagne's status as a global luxury commodity.

The Widow Clicquot's legacy lives on not only via the continuous success of her brand, but also through the innumerable lives she has touched. Her narrative serves as a strong reminder of how one person may have a significant impact on an industry and society. Barbe-Nicole's life and work exhibit resilience, ingenuity, and leadership, and provide vital lessons for today's entrepreneurs and business leaders. Her legacy continues to inspire, demonstrating that with vision and determination, even the most difficult hurdles can be overcome and greatness achieved.

As we wrap off our look at Barbe-Nicole Ponsardin Clicquot's life, it is evident that her achievements to the champagne industry and role as a pioneer for women in business are absolutely amazing. Her inventive techniques, dedication to quality, and strategic vision revolutionized the champagne industry, leaving a legacy that continues to inspire and influence. The narrative of Widow Clicquot exemplifies the power of resilience, inventiveness, and empowerment, highlighting her life and work's long-lasting impact. Barbe-Nicole Ponsardin Clicquot has cemented her legacy as one of the most significant individuals in the champagne industry and beyond.

Made in United States
Troutdale, OR
01/07/2025